Fragile Interludes
by
Jon Francis

Fragile Interludes

FRAGILE INTERLUDES

Life is short,
        and the things
        that are truly beautiful
are often
too far apart:

a summer day at the beach,
a sunset in the fall,
a walk through the forest
                or a meadow,
or a quiet rock
    to sit upon
and watch the day begin.

    But perhaps
the greatest beauty
that life can offer
are those moments of closeness
            with another
times of sensitivity,
of understanding and sharing—
the kinds and times,
    degrees and shades
of love.

These are the moments of closeness—
        The fleeting,
    fragile interludes.

for Nikki

BOLINAS BEACH

I remember this beach
and I remember you.
We spent a day here once,
long ago when we were children.

We lay on the sand
        and we danced in the surf,
and I played the guitar
                while you sang.
We ran, and played, and kissed,
but mainly we laughed;
                at ourselves,
                at the sun and the sea.
I guess we laughed mostly
because we enjoyed just living.

It's been years
        since that day on the beach
and people
        as they grow older,
seem to laugh not as much.
And often, when they do laugh,
        it's not a real laugh.
It's not like the full, free laughter
                of a child.

I hope you haven't grown up since then,
                        at least
not in that way.

Sometimes its nice,
        in the evening,
when you're all alone
or the others are all asleep
                or have gone.
Sometimes its nice to remember
the day that has just passed
                or yesterday
        or maybe a day long ago;
to just recall the beauty,
        the wonder,
        the little things that matter.
Those days will never come again you know.

It was a beautiful day today
        even though it did rain.
The coldness, the dampness, the wind,
                made lovers seem to be
even more in love
as they fled,
        tightly together,
from a sudden cloudburst
into the small cafe
and cuddled quietly
drinking a cup of coffee
                        or maybe,
                just watching the rain
melt into the bay.

Someone else was there today
                    alone,
watching the rain
and the lovers
and others;
                    laughing, running.
I talked to her for awhile,
maybe because I loved her
        or wanted to love her
            or could have loved her;
perhaps because she knew
                    about people
                and lovers
            and rain.
I don't know where she went.
I never asked her name.

Sometimes it's nice
        in the evening
            to remember
the beauty, the wonder,
the little things that matter,
the where,
            the why,
                    the when,
and sometimes a person
you'll never see again.

IT WAS A PRETTY DAY

It was a pretty day,
        that day in late March.
The air was cool,   crisp.
The sky was cold and gray.
And it rained a little,
                        I think.
But still
it was a pretty day.

We didn't do anything that day,
        nothing special anyway.
We sat on the porch
                for awhile.
And we took a walk
        in the afternoon.
We just talked about things,
        remembered and laughed about things.
I had almost forgotten your smile.

Finally, inevitably,
            the night came
with no stars, no moon.
It came
        for me
                too soon.
But then, all things pass.
Though still,
it had been a pretty day.

BUTTERFLY

The summers shine warm in Morning Star
and there are meadows with tall grass
                              and butterflies
          and sincere, gentle people
                         who laugh.
But the rains fall hard
                    when winter comes
and the winds blow cold,
and the butterflies leave.

I gave her my blue coat once
because it was new and warm,
                    and she didn't have one.
     I gave it to her
                    because I liked it so much
                              and because
I liked her a little bit more.

The summers shine warm in Morning Star
and there are meadows with tall grass
                              and butterflies
          and sincere, gentle people
                         who laugh.
But someday the rains will fall again
and the winds will blow cold,
and the butterflies will leave.

Whenever winter comes
          and wherever butterflies go
I hope there is someone,
someone who likes her a little bit more
                    than a long blue coat;
a blue coat that is new

and warm.

MEETING

Our meeting came sudden;
               upon the road—
sudden and unexpected
as meetings so often are.

At first I thought
that her world was far different
        than mine;
and she must have felt the same
                       about me.
And at first
little was said between us.

The day was still young then,
and the hills and valleys of Oregon
were just beginning to awaken
               and bloom
with the coming of spring.
And as the sun spread higher
                and warmer,
the land grew greener
        and softer;
and we began to talk
and to know one another.
           And soon
we realized how similar
our worlds really were.
And the day became long
        and pleasant.

Then later,
as the evening drew near,
we stopped.
And she went north to Portland
and I continued west
        for the coast.
And we smiled,
and waved to each other,

as we parted.

Perhaps each of us feels at times
that his world is far different
                and separate
from that of others.

But maybe,
if we took the time
   to know one another a little better,
we might realize
how similar we really are.

and our worlds might become brighter;

        and our meetings,
a little more together.

SUNSET

The sun always sets
   in a different way
      every day.

Sometimes it gently fades
    into the mist;
and the colors are yellow,
      orange and grey.
Or sometimes,
when the clouds are large and many,
it leaves in flashes
      and spreadings
of violet, and pink, and crimson.
   And then,
      at other times,
it just sinks slowly—
   unobstructed, unattended,
behind a mountain
or into the sea.

When the evening grows near
I always try to take the time
to go somewhere special—
   (somewhere quiet and secluded,)
to say goodbye to the sun:
to think back upon the day
    that it brought;
to offer my thanks;
   and to hope
that the day which it brings
to those across the sea
is just as beautiful—
   just as pleasant
   and warm
    and cheerful,
as the one that it gave to me.

A STRANGER AT HARRAH'S CLUB

She was young and she was beautiful.
And when she laughed
she did it openly, sincerely.
And she smiled at the others around her.
                    And he,
                as I look back,
was old and withered;
        disillusioned perhaps,
and tired.

She only looked at him once,
            for only a few seconds—
                    silently,
then she turned and continued the game.
And the others;
they watched him
    and talked about him
and exchanged messages of concern
as he died.

He was an old man
and no one knew him.
He was a stranger,
            as we all were.
And when he had been taken away
the others turned and continued the game,
                    pushing and shouting,
unconcerned, forgetting.

Only one was silent.
Only one tear fell.
And I wish I could have saved it
to remember a beautiful young girl
who loved to laugh
        and live and smile.
I wish I could have saved it
for her
and for an old man
who was a stranger
and no one knew.

for Diane

OURSELVES

People seem cold sometimes.
Even the best of friends
greet each other with a mere "hello"
    or "how have you been".
And so often,
            even lovers
are ashamed, or embarrassed
                to kiss
        or to hold hands;
to show their love
or to be themselves
in front of others.

It seems that too many people
have lost that tenderness—
    that quality of being themselves.
Too many people are afraid
    to show their emotions:
to say "I love you"
            when they do;
to say "I've missed you"
        when they have;
to be themselves
    and to show it,
honestly and sincerely,
openly and consistently.

You called my name today
and you ran to my arms;
            laughing and kissing,
        squeezing each other tightly.
And the others around,
they must have thought
        that we were lovers.
And some of them watched,
and some of them smiled,
                and some of them
            turned away.
And I guess that none of them
                    really knew
we were only friends;
            but still—
the very best,
the very dearest,
    of friends.

As time passes on
and as each of us grows older,
I hope we never lose
                that wonderful thing—
our friendship;
and that beautiful quality
                    of always

being ourselves.

SATURDAY NIGHT
AND SUNDAY DAY

  (–A phone call; late Saturday night–
 from the far southern coast.)
"I miss you."
"I've been thinking about you."
"I want to see you
   and talk to you."
"Can we meet somewhere on the coast–
     somewhere between us?"
 "Tomorrow at noon?"

–An extra change of clothes,
    a jug of wine;
a dozen hits of speed
 and five hundred miles
through a windy winter night,
to the beach at El Capitan

and a day with Susan.

–Walking together
  through the magical forest
 of cypress and eucalyptus.
Skipping, running, laughing
    by the surf.
 Lying in the sand–

talking, wondering, thinking.

  –An unusually warm,
    gentle, november breeze–
a myriad of sizes and types,
 and shapes and depths
of clouds   and rocks;
and seas, and trees.
–The air, the beach, the sky–
some white,
 some blue,
  some gray;
And a sun–
 (a sun at play)
that sometimes goes
and sometimes stays.

–A number shared in the sunset:
 to mellow the shadows of evening,
   to enhance the colors of the sky;
to think back softly
       upon the day,
and to smile.

–A night roaming the streets of Isla Vista,
        (a sandwich in a delicatessen)–
window-wishing
by the fronts of the little shops.

     Then a final hour together,
   on the beach at El Capitan–

(the lights upon the sea,
   the wind in the trees;
The moon through the clouds–
                  on our bodys–
   on the sand).

        –An embrance–
                  long, intense–
        a kiss;
The sorrows of leaving,
   and the words that lovers say
when they must say goodbye.

Then back in the night:
through the fog and wind,
           and misty-type rain–
500 miles
to the mountains of the north.

Back to the hours and weeks
        of being alone;
 of thinking of someone
lying heavy on your mind,
                and waiting–

 waiting for a phone call
late in the night.

IN NEATLY WRAPPED PACKAGES

Do you recall
   a stormy September day,
when the winds blew angry
                  and scattered
      from the east;
and the rain fell thick through the fog,
and I stopped at your little cafe
for a cup of coffee
   and something warm to eat?

I remember how I tried to smile
                  and be friendly to you;
but you reacted only coldly—
   (as if I were intruding).

And you wiped the counter
      and cleared the tables
         and stacked the dishes
   in a grey, detached-type way;
and spoke only those words
that were necessary.

Perhaps it was the cut of my clothes,
         my beard,
   or the long hair
that caused you to act as you did?

Or maybe you were just too busy
to be friendly?

People today seem far too distant
                from one another.
There is too deep a lack of understanding;
        compassion, and togetherness
to be overly concerned
                with the quality of one's clothes
or the length of one's hair.

Perhaps by now you have changed.
                        I surely hope so.

Perhaps now you know
that life is too uncertain
        and closeness is too distant
to ever be too busy
to be friendly–

and that things of beauty
                        and worth
do not always come
in neatly wrapped packages.

SOMETHING WONDERFUL

There's something wonderful
about music or songs;
              laughter or silence:
the sound of the rain,
the feel of the wind,
the touch of the sun,
              and people—
      (gentle, sincere people);
or a smile from a stranger,
or the greeting of a friend.

There's something beautiful
about the sunlight
              in the morning:
the clouds in the sky,
the stars in the night,
the flowers and forests and meadows
                    in the springtime;
or a sunset in the evening,
or a fire in the night-time.

And there's something marvelous
              about the fury of a storm:
the anger of the thunder;

the peacefulness at noon,
or the mellow of a summer.

There's something wonderful—
something pure and good and beautiful
    about the little things:
the quiet things and quiet times in life.

There's something about them
                    that makes them
a most important
and most precious

part of life.

A DAY

Another day has passed.
Another piece of life
        has come and gone.
And nothing was learned
and nothing was lost.
And no decisions were made
and no courses were charted
It was just a day that came
                and stayed
and then went.

I use to worry about days,
        and hours, and minutes;
as if they were too important
to be just lived–
        to be just enjoyed.
They are important you know,
but not too important to be lived
        or to be enjoyed.

The sun rose this morning
and the day that it brought was sunny
        and warm and beautiful,
and the birds sang.
And when the sun set,
the evening breezes were cool
        and quiet.
And nothing was learned
and nothing was lost.
And no decisions were made
and no courses were charted.
It was just a day
        that came
    and stayed
and went.
But to me it was a most important day.
It was an entire day spent
                alone,

together
in love
with you.

BROTHERS

The sun is falling
into the pale western sea.
    And here,
   by the shores of San Francisco,
people are rushing homeward–
           worn and weary:
watching the day ending,
   the sun setting;

looking forward to the evening,
their precious measure of quiet
            and tranquility,
and the seclusion of sleep.

     And there,
   somewhere across the sea,
others are just awaking–
        refreshed and optimistic:
seeing the day beginning,
   the sun rising;

contemplating the hours ahead
and the work that must be done.

We are all brothers—
all children upon the same tiny planet;
    separated only by water,
            mountains, deserts,
        or a few hours time.
And though our colors—
    our customs or languages—
are somewhat different;
our loves and desires,
our basic goals,
            fears and necessities
are forever the same.

But how blind,
how suspicious and apprehensive,
        have we become:
confined by the pettiness of ourselves
    and the narrowness of our minds;
estranged by malignant concepts
        of politics,
            economics, and nationalities;
marshalled by the sick, twisted
                maneuverings and propaganda
of numerous governmental factions
striving madly for control
and infinite power.

Our destiny has not been premade.
The choice between peace or anguish,
    future prosperity or annihilation,
    for ourselves
        and for those to follow,
lies crucially
within our hands.

If we are ever to know
        the magnificent potential which is mans';
if we are to go on toward unity,
                            peace and progress,
        which are so possible
            and so very essential
we must learn quickly
to look with rationality
        at ourselves,
            our earth,
and at those around us.

We must obliterate the senseless forms of alienation
                        that divide us
and come together as one.

                    But first,
                most important,
we must become fully
        and forever aware
that basically
we are all the same–

All children upon the same small earth;

    all brothers
under the same glorious sun.

Something more than friends

BLUE-GREY

A late-noon mist lies heavy
        throughout the valley,
and the evening sun
is only slightly visible.
Blue-grey lies the lake
                and the sky.
And the mountains, and the trees, and the rocks
                that encircle
are dark:
        dark and solemn
in tones of blue
and shades of grey.

It's the kind of time,
        (the type of day),
that makes one feel lonely
    and sad somehow:
a little more mellow,
understanding perhaps
and tolerant.

And somewhere,
        below,
where the mountains reach into the lake
you are probably feeling,
        as I—
the moods and thoughts,
the shades and impressions
        of blue
and grey.

I'm going to come to you tonight:
because I regret the sadness
        that has passed between us,
because I've missed you,
        and because
there is already too much hurt and sorrow
                in life as it is
to ever be the cause
of any more.

LOVERS

His hair was long, and blond,
         and her's
was just as long;   silkin and black.
The winter was mild that year
         and at night
the skies were clear
and the stars were many.

They met upon the road-
one was heading north
      and the other, south.
One smiled
  and the other said hello.
And through the time that followed
they were together.

By day they loved on the beaches
or roamed or' the meadows
                  or hillsides;
and at night,   they cuddled close
in sheltered caves
or wooded coves.

And no questions were asked
and no promises were spoken.
No tales were told
and no excuses were given.
         and their love
was young, open and beautiful.
And they laughed at the darkness;
and kissed in the sunlight.

And when their time had passed,
            they parted:
without regret, or guilt, or sorrow.

Only remembering perhaps;
but warmly,
            more complete now,
      and happily.

And one went north
and one went south.

A CERTAIN FEELING

I have a certain feeling for you;
a very beautiful, special,
                unique kind of feeling.
And although I've wanted to;
I've never told you.

I guess because,
I didn't know how to say it.

(No one has ever given it a name.)

It's that inbetween feeling;

lying somewhere
after friendship ends,

                    and before
love begins.

BECAUSE IT WAS YOUR BIRTHDAY

I wanted to be with you tonight.
I wanted to be there
        for the party we'd planned;
to see the surprise in your eyes,
to hear you laugh
                and cry.
I knew that you would cry.
You always cry when you're really happy.
And I wanted to be with you,
because you mean so much to me,
and because it was your birthday.

The past year had been rough,
                as all years are
        when one pursues a star.
There are mountains to climb
                and between them,
endless deserts, plains and fields.
There are rivers to cross
        on bridges one builds.

You had climbed those mountains,
                each to its hilt.
You had crossed those rivers
                on bridges you'd built.
And I wanted to be with you,
to share the joy of your victory
and because it was your birthday.

I wanted to be with you tonight
                and I was,
although from afar.
I laughed with you and I cried.
And I was happy for you,
        so very happy,
because of the things you had done
and the things that you stand for,
because you mean so much to me
and because it was your birthday.

31

for mlr

WE'LL MEET AGAIN

I've never kissed you
    or even held your hand.
We've only been together a few times.
        But even at that,
I know I could love you,
and I know that you
    could love me.

But places call you
and another lies deep in your heart.
And others, and places,
    call me.

I won't kiss you tonight
and I won't hold your hand.
Nor will you - I.

We both understand.

Perhaps someday
    we'll meet again,
when hearts are freer,
when minds are clearer.

Someday we'll meet again;
if not you,
        another you;
if not I,
        another I.

Someday we'll meet again,
when hearts are freer,
when minds are clearer.

for Linda

THE VERY BEST OF FRIENDS

I find it hard to say goodbye
            after five and a half years.
And I guess you probably do to.

But it has to be you know.
We were only children when we were married;
                        alone, unhappy, afraid,
and clinging to each other
because there was no one else.

We've grown up since then,
but in different ways entirely.
I'm not happy in your world,
nor are you happy in mine.

Let's just say
            that we were childhood sweethearts;
that we laughed and kissed
                        and that we sometimes cried;
and that somewhere, in-someway, at sometime,
            we loved.

Let's just say it like it was.
And if we can,
let's try to always be
the very best of friends.

ONA

Her name was Ona
and she was from Norway.
Her uncle had settled in Oregon
        some ten or twelve years ago,
and now he owned some little cabins
just down the beach
from where I was staying.
And she had come to spend her summer vacation.

I had noticed her often
                upon the beach;
always alone:
looking for shells or pretty pebbles,
running lightly through the surf,
        or sitting quietly–
watching the shifting patterns
                of the sky,
                        the sea.
And one day I walked up to her
and said hello.

She smiled,
        then nodded and hesitated,
and spoke something in Norwegian
which meant about the same
as hello.
And through the weeks that followed
our time was spent together:

playing on the beaches
        meadows and hillsides;
laughing with the summer skies
or walking softly
beneath the stars.

And though she knew nothing of English,
                nor I of Norwegian;
we quickly grew to know
        and understand one another,
in a most clear and beautiful manner.
For nothing was wanted,
        demanded or expected
from either.
And because of our barrier
deception or lies seemed impossible.
And to some extent perhaps,
we started to love.

Our communication was simple and direct:
a touch of the arm; the pointing of a finger;
an expression,   gesture,
        symbol or motion;
silence or laughter.

And sometimes we spoke
the few small words
we had learned together.

But perhaps we revealed ourselves best
                by the vibrations,
    understandings and thought-waves,
that flowed between us.
        (Those silent statements from deep within
            that are so constant,
            and so very difficult to hide or disquise.)
Sometimes I feel that our awareness,
        our knowledge
                and understanding of one another,
was far more complete and sincere
than that between many
who live the same lives
and speak the same language.

And when the summer had ended
she flew back to Norway
        and I drove south to Mexico,
where a summer was just beginning
all over again.

for Olivia

IT WAS SAD

I walked down the hall with you today;
        your arm in mine,
        your eyes on the floor ahead of you.
And I watched silently
while you were married.

It was sad somehow.
Perhaps because I felt about you once,
        and you felt so much for me.
Or perhaps because
it was a beautiful sunny day,
like that day so long ago
when you thought the world had ended
                        and you cried
                beside his coffin.
Or maybe just because of you;
        all the things you never had,
        and all the things
that you should have had.

I'm glad though.
And I'm happy for you.
        But still,
                somehow,
it was sad.

WILL YOU LOOK BACK

Somewhere ahead there lies a plateau;
Somewhere above the fog,   the mist
                 and irrationality.
A place where the sun shines bright
            and there are no clouds.
A place where life and truth and meaning
             are known and understood.

And things are seen
for what they are.

I've come a long way in the years past.
             Alone mostly.
I've struggled up many a steep trail
and climbed some distant mountains
                    that once
        I never thought I could.
And I've learned so very much
about so many different things.

And once,
        when I had stopped to rest,
I looked back and saw you.
I called your name,
            reached down, and helped you up.
I taught you how to climb
and what to search for.

You climb well,
and you learn quickly.
And I'm happy
          and something more
than proud of you.

If ever it should happen
that you reach that plateau before I
will you stop and look back?
If you should get there before I
would you call my name?
Would you reach down to me?
        Will you remember
and will you help me up?

NOW

I never knew you
                 before today.
Oh, we had spent time together.
We had gone places and done things.
We had even spoken,
     but always in a hurry,
                  superficially.
I really didn't know you.
And I guess that you
       really didn't know me.

We were like so many others;
            two people
doing things together,
laughing, joking,
playing, kissing,
     holding hands,
                     sometimes.

We just never stopped
     to know each other.

We should have.

Today we didn't do anything,
nothing that could be seen anyway.
We just sat
        in the sand.
And we talked.
We watched the sea gulls above us
and the tiny sails so far away,
the surf, the sun, the sand around us
                        AND
            for the first time
we talked.

I'm happy for today
I'm happy because
        I might never have known you
            and you might never have known me,
and because
                I love you
                                    now.

for D. D.

SOMETHING MORE THAN FRIENDS

I never thought that I would miss you,
or that I would think too often about you
                        once you had gone.
And I guess it was because
we are only friends.

We've always been just friends,
   and never lovers.

But the weeks have passed since then
and I've thought of you frequently:

I've thought of sun-filled days
                        and sea gulls,
            and afternoon strolls
                  along the surf—
   (the life, and love, and laughter
                        inside you).

I've thought of slow-type days,
               when the rains came—
days when we'd sit by the fire
and discuss the world
               we had been born into;
right and wrong,
   good and evil,
and the people
            around us—
   (your sincerity, concern,
                  and sensitivity).

And I've thought about the day that you left
and the tears that were in your eyes.

I know how very much you love the coast:
   the feel of the wind,
   and the taste of the salt
                    in the air;
the tiny towns,
the quiet beaches,
and the gentle, beautiful people
                that live there.

And I know how dearly you love the sea.

But sometimes
         I think that maybe,
                       or partly,
      why you were sad
was because we were saying goodbye;
and because you feel,
                  like I do,
that somehow;
                in some way;
we are
   and will always be

something more than friends.

for Mary

I DEDICATE "THE SEA"

To you,
in memory of Santa Cruz:
the days and nights by the sea;
        the moments, the minutes,
                            the hours;
laughing and kissing and loving
                        in the sun,
                beneath the stars;
    on the sand.
And sometimes,
just walking alone,
                    together.
        The movements of your body.
        The sounds of the sea.

To you,
in memory of the mornings:
                    silent
    except for birds and breezes.
And the sun between the curtains.
And you,
lying asleep
        or awake
in my arms.
        naked and beautiful,
        and in love.

To you,
I dedicate "The Sea":
in memory of the love you felt for me
                    and the love
            that I felt for you.
And also,
    knowing,
that the sea lives on
                and only you
        and I
have gone.

*Love
is selfish*

LOVE IS SELFISH

Love is selfish you know.
It's the most selfish thing there is.
It's wanting to be with someone,
wanting to hold and touch someone,
wanting to do things
        to make that someone happy,
and wanting that someone to want you;

because the wanting,
        the holding, the touching,
the wanting to make happy;
just having that someone
makes you happy.

Lets's be selfish,

together.

TODAY

Today,
While you were away,
I made the bed and washed the dishes.
I vacuumed the living room rug
        and ironed your cotton blouses.
I did a hundred little chores,
a hundred things
I never liked to do;
things I did for you,
        and for me
because I love you.

You called later in the day
and said that Dion was fine,
that Sam was still away,
that you'd be home by nine.

It snowed just before dark
and I shoveled out the driveway
so that you'd have a place to park.
I split some logs
out beside the house
and started a fire
        just before nine,
then sat and waited
                    for you
              to again
be mine.

GLENBROOK BAY

It's almost three o'clock now
on a bright August day
and I'm sitting alone
                on the shores
of Glenbrook Bay.

I came here today
        to be alone.
Just to be alone
        and to think.
And because I had to be alone.
You were asleep.

There's something about an August day,
                or any day,
that's beautiful.
Any day without obligations,
        without need to come or go,
a day free to laugh or run or play,
and sometimes a day
                to just sit and think.

I've thought today,
about you mostly
    and some about me.
I thought about your smile
      and your laughter,
sometimes your seriousness.
I just thought about you
and all the things I like about you.

The wind is picking up now
and the sun has sparkled the water
    with a million silver glitters.

The water talks to me sometimes you know,
      and the waves
        and the wind also.
They talk to me
especially when I'm alone,
      and they know,
they know how much I miss you
and how desperately I want you.

And what was a perfect day
isn't perfect somehow
    when I'm alone
and without you.

YOU SMILED

You smiled once,
and I smiled back.
And once I loved you.
And once you loved me.

It came
and it was beautiful
and then it left.

Sometimes I wish you had never smiled,
        that we had never been in love.
Sometimes I wish I could have gone on
and never have known you.

But maybe it's better to have known you
                        and loved you—
        even to have cried.
Maybe it's better to have loved,
                    if only once,
than not at all.

At least I know now
        what love is.

And I never knew
before you smiled.

HAPPY,
YET SAD

Today you are a person:
          beautiful,
               alive,
         and sincere.

Yesterday you were nothing.

And I'm happy for you,
         yet sad;

happy that you've become a person,
                     and sad

that I knew you yesterday

and not today.

IF IT IS POSSIBLE

If it is possible
    that there are times
when I love you more
than at other times;
then it must be in the winter.

It must be when the mist
        drifts thick and grey:
over the mountains,
across the meadow,
    and through the tops
of the trees–
and your soft singing,
        your laughter,
        your gentle glow,
seem so much more beautiful
in comparison.

It must be
when the rains fall heavy:
pounding on the roof,
rattling the windows
        and shutters,
and we are lying by the fire–
      kissing, touching, loving–
and your closeness, and warmth
seem so much more intense.

If it is possible
    that there are times
when I love you more
than at other times;
then it must be in the winter.

It must be in the winter,
if it is possible.

YOUR LOVE PLEASES ME

Your love pleases me.
It has made my life happier than
    if I had never known you.
And each thing that you do;
each smile,
a wave of your hand,
a glance from your eye,
the winds breeze in your hair,
    All that is you
has made my life happy.

If each person,
    each moment or situation,
each ray of light,
each sight or sound
                or taste
        or breath—

if all that is life
can bring such happiness

can there be anymore?

How late is it?

It seems like I've been asleep for days
or that I haven't held you in years.

Let's make love
        until the sun shines.
We can sleep tomorrow,
            or next week.

There's always time for sleep.

Something to hold on to

SOMETHING TO HOLD ON TO

I guess that each of us
    must, at times,
have something solid
to hold on to:
(a goal perhaps,
          or an ideal);
or maybe another
  or the dream,
     or hope,
        or memory
of another?

When the days grow misty
and the loneliness within
           seems unbearable
I turn and look at you,
    (or all that I still have of you)—

a footprint,
traced in crayon,
on the wall of my van.

It's all that I still have of you.

It's my little something
to hold on to.

NEW YORK, 1964

A city: cold, impersonal, lonely;
and three thousand miles from home.

Two young boys:
                dirty, disgusted;
        shunned, harassed, and scorned;
                    almost hopeless—
looking for an idea,
    a memory
        or dream
  of youth—
Looking for America.

        And a man
        of seventy, or seventy-five;
a man who had traveled the oceans,
known the rivers and plains and mountains
who understood
                and cared
where others only glanced
  or stared—
                unknowing.
A man who called himself Michael Lohan.

And this man from Ireland—
        this man of America—
opened his door,.
  reached out his arms,
and bid them welcome.

And in a city:
    cold, impersonal and lonely;
two young boys:
            feeling lost, disgusted,
    almost hopeless;
stopped—
    and stayed—
  laughed, lived, and smiled.

And again,
    for a time at least,

America was real.

BY MYSELF

It was winter then,
   and in the mornings
the dew lay heavy in the meadows
               and the fog,
         that was the sky,
drifted silently through the redwoods.
   And in the evenings
the winds often blew
and the rains sometimes fell.
                  And always,
it was cold and damp.

I was alone that winter;
      as I almost always am;
and I was hiding,
            behind wooden walls:
from the fog
     and the rain
         and the cold,
and inside
I was hiding from myself—
                  from others;
perhaps I was hiding
even from life.

Then once,
     in the beginning of the night,
she knocked upon my door.
And warmed her body by the fire
                  and smiled
            and stayed
till winter had gone away.

And between the rain
                  and wind and fog
she gave me answers
      to questions
I'd not before known.
And she planted within me
a bit of hope,
      and meaning and worth,
then disappeared
            once again
      with a smile
in the beginning of the night.

It's winter again,
   and in the mornings
the dew lays heavy in the meadows
                  and the fog,
            that is the sky,
drifts silently through the redwoods.
   And in the evenings
the winds often blow
and the rains sometimes fall.
                  And always,
it is cold and damp.

But I don't hide anymore.
I walk through the fog
                  and the forests;
   along the country roads
      and by the sea shore.
And sometimes I think of her
            and all that she gave me:
and although there's no one with me,
I'm not alone anymore–

I'm just by myself.

WITH MOUNTAINS TO CLIMB
AND SEA SHORES TO WALK

There's a butterfly in the garden.
          (He's just playing out there)
jumping from flower to flower,
feeling the summer breeze on his wings
                    and the morning sunlight
          on his back.
And now and then
he stops for a little rest
          on a blade of grass,
     or a fence post, or a flower petal.

You are beautiful;
          as beautiful as butterflies in a garden,
          as warm as morning sunlight.
And your heart is gentle,
as pure, as gentle,
          as summer breezes
              or green grass
     or flower petals.
But you don't smile like the sunlight
and you don't laugh like the breezes.
And,
          although you should be,
you are not happy like the butterflies.

Life shouldn't be over at fifteen.
        It wasn't meant that way.
At fifteen it has only begun.
At fifteen there are mountains to climb
            and picnics to be had,
there is sunlight
and birds that sing
        and songs to be sung.
At fifteen there are sea shores to walk,
                    shells to be found,
                    and sweethearts to be loved
And at fifteen,
            especially at fifteen,
there should be hope,
belief and faith
            in the future
        and in good people.
There should always be hope
for the beautiful things in life
no matter how hard
they so often are to find.

If I could,
    and if you'd let me,
I would climb those mountains with you
and walk along the sea shore.
And if I could
I'd take your lifeless little needle,
break it into a million pieces
        and bury it in the sand
or scatter it
upon the oceans.

I don't think you would miss it much,
                    at least
not with mountains to climb,
songs to sing,
and sea shores to walk.

HOW MUCH?

The night is cold.
And the winds
        that comes from the east
are strong
and chilling.

        But perhaps,
things are not as bad
as they could be.

The moon is full,
and the light that it gives
    is more than enough
for the simple things
        that must be done.

And there's a fire before us
that is gay and warm.
A lake beside us
        to watch,
            to listen to;
a sack of bread and cheese—
            a blanket,
and a rock behind
to lean our heads upon.

How much does it really take
        to be happy—
            to be content?
—some warmth, some light;
a little comfort, a little food;
the beauty of nature before us
and the quiet of the night
        to enfold us.

        And,

a kiss from you
and a squeeze from me.

YOUR LIFE

Your life lies as a panorama
unfolding before you.

Ahead there are mountains and valleys—
     deserts, oceans, meadows.
And the roads—the choices,
        are many;
and their ends—their results,
     are often distant and varied.
There might come happiness or sorrow;
    mere contentment or total fulfillment;
pacifity, envolvement,
exultation or regret.

     But always,
  until one has reached the height of his aspirations
there must be change.

Choose your roads carefully.
Be cautious, analytical;
     and free, and flexible within yourself.
Try to anticipate all that might lie ahead.
And if your choice ever happens to lead
to something less than what was expected
      feel not too discouraged,
    remorseful or defeated.
Leave it and choose another.
For through experience
one's knowledge does usually broaden;
      and often,
the second road is far more promising
than could have been the first.

  Maintain hope, confidence, and resolution.
       And remember always;
that he who stays within a desert
     when he yearns for the sea
grows gradually deeper
in frustration and regret,
   and in the end perishes—

having hardly lived at all.

for Sue Wilcox

SOMETIMES IN THE DAYTIME

Sometimes in the daytime
when I'm walking alone
            through the countryside,
or sitting quietly
    by the meadow at my doorstep;
and the sun is shining
and the grasses and the flowers
                    are growing
and the sound of the surf
            seems distant,
        yet near,
I think of you.

And sometimes,
                then,
I might hear the whisper
of your guitar;
the drifting softness of your voice,
the tranquility and beauty
                    in your heart,
and the wholeness of your sincerity.

Sometimes in the daytime
I think of you,
and recall all the wonder
        that you are;
and when I do,
    I smile,
and I feel within
        a kind of peace,
                a contentness—
a certain serenity
that only comes

sometimes in the daytime.

NEAR WHERE THE COTTONWOODS GROW

If you walk down by the river
 and around the bend,
   (near where the cottonwoods grow)
you can see the moon.

It's almost full tonight
and the clouds that drift before it
      are scattered and fluffy.
Some of them are thin and transparent;
and others are thicker—
    more solid and darker.

And if you wade out to the Rock,
and look up the river toward the south,
you can see Horsetail Falls.
It's a ribbon of metallic brilliance
 in a setting of mountain-black.

And the dancing waters before you
            glow on their crests
       and sparkle.
And the evening breeze
touches lightly upon your face.

There are perhaps
a billion beautiful places on this earth;
      a hundred delicate times of day,
  and a thousand enchanting kinds of night.

We can't really see
            or know
all the wonders of this world;
for life is too demanding
and we haven't the time.

We can only enjoy
      and give thanks
for that which is ours.

Come, let's go together;
down by the river and around the bend,
  (near where the cottonwoods grow)

We can see the moon.

SOMETHING ABOUT HER

I was alone at the time
and there was no one else
        in San Francisco
that I knew.

But it wasn't really loneliness,
            or sorrow,
        or need-of-company
that brought me to her.

It was something about her:
something about her eyes,
                her smile—
        her softness and serenity:
the things that she said
and the way that she said them.

        And partly I guess,
it was something about me—
something about me
            and my knowing:
knowing that in the morning
            or in the evening
        or late in the night—
knowing that she would be there,
                awake and waiting,
    happy to see me
            and glad
    that I had come;

And knowing especially
that the days
        and the nights
        that followed
would be a little easier,
            a little brighter;
because of San Francisco,
because of the night,

        and because of something
about her.

OUTSIDE
AND INSIDE

The rains fall heavy
          on the northern coast.
And in the winter;
the mist hangs low
          and shrouds the mountains
                    and the sea;
and the trees,
               across the meadow,
are veiled
in gray.

If I look out my window
I see only sorrow,
          gloom and obscurity.

And if I turn,
and look inside,
          I see you;
and the rain is laughing,
and the mist beyond
               is beautiful

and sunny.

THE PREACHER

I met him where he sat—
before the entrance to the cave
                    in which he lived.
His hair and beard
were both long and dark.
His face spoke of knowledge and tranquility,
and his eyes
        shone brilliant and transparent.

And with him lived his woman, Karen;
and their dog, Seaborn.

He was known thereabouts
        as "The Preacher";
and that he most certainly was,
though not at all
of the classical sense.
For his words were never of God
                        or the Devil,
        or of punishment or sin,
                or heaven or damnation.
They were slow and gentle:
of the oneness and beauty of nature,
        in all her hours
    and all her seasons;
the role of man—
the rewards of peace and contentment—
            within that oneness;

    and sometimes
he would turn toward Karen,
squeeze her in his arm,
        and tell softly
of man and woman;
the joys of togetherness and love,
being two instead of one,
and of understanding
    and tenderness.

We spent that day together—
   sitting in the sand:
speaking of things
we each felt precious and beautiful;
watching the autumn clouds
roll slowly across the beach;
      and sipping the tea
          of spices and hemp
that Karen kept simmering
upon the fire.

And as I left,
   and through the days that followed,
I knew a certain peace
         and understanding—
a certain togetherness and tranquility
          that never
have I gotten from any sermon
nor from within the walls
of any church.

UPON THE MOON

They say if you wish
upon the first star that shines,
your wish will always
come true.

I saw the moon first tonight,
       while the sky was still clear
                      and blue.
It rose above the hills,
       long before the stars;
before even the sun
had begun to set.
And so I made a wish upon it.

But I must not tell you, you know,
for that would certainly
          break the spell
and then the wish
might never come true.

But perhaps I can say
that it had to do with you
                   and with me,
and with the time
we will be spending together.
Perhaps I can say
       that it was hopeful
and sincere.

And perhaps,
       just maybe,
a wish upon the moon
is better
     and more probable
than a wish
upon a star.

for Joan Baez

THANK YOU

Thank you:
for the songs you sung in the morning,
    when I awoke—
stumbling with the sleep and trust of youth
    still in my eyes:
confused, bewildered, disillusioned,
and grasping desperately
for something to cling to—
            to give me hope;
to believe in,
to begin with.

Thank you:
for the smiles you gave—
            the encouragement;
when the sun was high
and the birds were singing,
    and I wanted someone to associate with:
some form of beauty to relate to—
to give me strength,
to share with.

Thank you:
for the words you spoke in the evenings;
when I was tired and discouraged
and needed comforting, cheering,
        and consolation—
reassurance
  to end a trying day,
to hope for a better tomorrow.

Thank you
for being sensitive,   concerned and true;
  for being intransigent and courageous.
And thank you,
            the very most of all,
for being yourself—
  (so beautiful, so sincere)
and for helping me
to be myself.

24 BESSIE STREET

It was in an older part of the city;
    where the hills rose gradually
and the streets were narrow–
        cracked and crumbling–
a part of the city that was now forgotten.

The houses were of wood,
   weathered and worn;
leaning mournfully against one another:
like tombstones from the past,
or veterans of wars gone-bye:
  too tired to stand
                 or march,
too old to smile,
and too proud
  to cry.

They had been young once,
perhaps the heart of the city–
  the glory of their time–
but that time was long ago.
And now their colors had gone
            or faded,
their bones seemed twisted
   and withered;
and their souls
seemed shattered.

It was the third from the corner
and looked no different from the others;
      except perhaps,
that the second-story windows
were clear and sparkling–
with sills and frames of glossy orange.
  And above the door
hung a little red, yellow, and white sign
              that read,
"24 Bessie".

And within
there was music,
        sunshine and gaiety;
with walls like rainbows–
orange, green, and pink;
    yellow and blue–
and pictures of children, lakes,
    and springtime meadows.
And flowers smiled
in every corner
of every room.

And there,
        within this shell of beauty,
there lived an angel–
an angel in faded old blue jeans,
a plain, loose-fitting T-shirt;
  barefeet, or sandals:

an angel–
with not a trace of falsehood or evil
    within her heart
    or mind or soul:
an angel–
pouring forth happiness,
                love and goodwill;
  being it, showing it, causing it;
because she herself
was really,
completely happy.

Often would I stop there,
when the turmoil of the city became too much
  or nights were lonely
    or days grew misty.
And her door was always open.
And the world within
        knew neither day nor night.
And loneliness, sorrow, or depression
seemed suddenly impossible,
                banned,
            or reduced to a triviality.

And the others that I knew there
were both gentle and sincere.

She's gone now,
and 24 Bessie St.
    isn't the same.
The windows are cracked and stained.
The ledges lie dark with soot.
And the little red, yellow, and white sign
                     above the door
has disappeared.
And the people who now live there
      will tell you
what an evil, degenerate person she was:
that she held parties late into the night;
used marijuana and other drugs;
how she had finally been caught
      and sent to prison,
"where God knows she certainly belongs";
and that,
"the world is better off without the likes of her".

And they stand in her doorway
              squalid and unkempt;
staring with suspicious, beady-type eyes;
hiding beneath their blind,
    pre-conditioned self-righteousness.
And the rooms behind
  are dark and lifeless.
Pieces of plaster lie upon the floor.
The walls of orange and green
             and yellow and blue
  are whitewashed,
        stained and disfigured.
And articles of clothing,
            beer cans
            and discarded magazines,
gather cobwebs and dirt
in the corners
where flowers once smiled.

Sometimes in the evening
I walk through the streets of the city,
    or watch the sunset over the bay.
                        And often
        I think of her–
because I remember how she loved the sunset,
                        and because I know
                    that where she is
there are no sunsets.
And rainbows never shine
on grey cement walls.
And flowers or music or laughter
        cannot live
in dark forsaken holes.

And I feel the urge
to scream
  or cry.

Wendy, I love you;
    as did all those that knew you–
as would anyone
                who hopes for beauty,
                    innocence and sincerity.
I love you,
and I hope, and I pray
that the injustice that has been done
        will not change you;
that you retain all the goodness–
            all the laughter and gentleness–
that you once were;
that you grow neither bitter nor revengefull,
                    and that soon
                the day will come
when innocence and beauty–
when life, happiness, and gaiety–
are no longer feared   or repressed;
for angels upon this earth are rare;
and they are needed,   especially now,
        by all of us–

whether we realize it or not.

SUNDAY

When you were young
did you remember Sundays?
They always seemed to be
        the happiest day of the week.
There was church in the morning
and a big family breakfast afterwards
                with cinnamon toast
                        and coffee cake,
and rides in the country
and visits to the zoo.

But Sunday's not the only happy day.
There are Mondays and Tuesdays
        when the sun shines.
There are Wednesdays or Saturdays
                        or Fridays,
and even Thursdays can be happy.

Let's make Wednesdays into Tuesdays
        and Fridays into Mondays,
And if we can
let's try to make everyday
        a Sunday.